About the Author

I have a strong passion for making people laugh and smile, my other passion is expressing raw and sometimes intrusive emotions through lyrics, music and poetry. I constantly fall short of my own aspirations, and that's something that is going to end, because I'm here to stay. With that, I figured I'd start sending a little madness and weirdness everybody's way.

Self-Induced Regicide

Ryan Blair

Self-Induced Regicide

Olympia Publishers
London

www.olympiapublishers.com
OLYMPIA PAPERBACK EDITION

Copyright © Ryan Blair 2022

The right of Ryan Blair to be identified as author of
this work has been asserted in accordance with sections 77 and 78
of the Copyright, Designs and Patents Act 1988.

All Rights Reserved

No reproduction, copy or transmission of this publication
may be made without written permission.
No paragraph of this publication may be reproduced,
copied or transmitted save with the written permission of the
publisher, or in accordance with the provisions
of the Copyright Act 1956 (as amended).

Any person who commits any unauthorised act in relation to
this publication may be liable to criminal
prosecution and civil claims for damage.

A CIP catalogue record for this title is
available from the British Library.

ISBN: 978-1-80074-400-4

This is a work of fiction.
Names, characters, places and incidents originate from the writer's
imagination. Any resemblance to actual persons, living or dead, is
purely coincidental.

First Published in 2022

Olympia Publishers
Tallis House
2 Tallis Street
London
EC4Y 0AB

Printed in Great Britain

Dedication

I dedicate this book to my loved ones, who refused to let me give up on myself.

Acknowledgements

Thank you to my good friends, Carter, Marshall and David for believing in me and helping me hone my craft. I love you all immensely.

I'm a 26… thousand-year-old, feeling 26 years old, creator. I've got an amazing sense of humor and a passion for making people laugh and smile. My other passion is expressing raw and sometimes intrusive emotions through lyrics, music, or poetry. I constantly fall short of my own aspirations, and that's something that is going to end, 'cause I'm here to stay, so I'm going to send a little madness and weirdness everybody's way.

So, paint my thoughts across the bedroom wall,
I wasn't built in a day yet that's all it took to fall,
Paint my thoughts across the fucking wall,
Cause I'm over this life,
I'm over it all.

This solace is all I could ask for,
This grievance is all but my own,
I find that I bend over backwards,
Always just to go and end up alone.
I left the house, I left my home,
In search of dignity and hope,
Overproof just to cope,
You know what they say—
When in Rome.

So, I let this cheap distillate taste,
Fill the void you left in place,
But it's no use, I couldn't tell you the last time I was sober.
Still, I'm wasted wasting away,
So I let these cancerous gusts fill my sails,
I wail to the gallows,
Vagabond,
If not forever further on.

Silence floods the empty space between the lobes,
Displacing the cancer feasting on your hope,
Well, I sit and watch a whisper kiss a claymore,
Putrefying all we've come to know.
Broken glass and dispatched bottle caps,
Half-assed liquor lullabies and cold sweat whiskey naps,
An instant can change your life,
Don't fuck with a sober mind,
Bask in the morning light,
Let it lick the sores of last night's wounded optimist.

This reputation stains a platinum presence,
Dismantles any adolescence briefly present,
For a pocket of joy will cast no shadow in this life,
Omnipotent sorrow, cheers, rejoice.

Is this everything that I can be?
A vivid nightmare deconstructing everything I've built.
Is this everything that once was sweet?
'Cause this bitterness permeates my soul,
Petrifying silhouettes of shadows deemed non-vacant.

Raise a glass to mandated melancholy misinterpreted as meekness,
To the vagabonds and hopeless wandering sleepless,
'Cause I'm at my weakest the first fucking day the week hits,
And I guess you didn't mean it 'cause you said you'd never leave, but you weren't here to see this
Bloody mess as I'm astral beside the carcass,
And, Darling, to my attest this pile of flesh it had my scent.

With eyes of brimstone, you left me craving sin,
Oh, peculiar little creature, if only I'd known,
How sinister your intentions truly were,
You shot me a gaze and I couldn't help but hold on,
Oh God, if only I'd been aware,
The gilded beauty of a gorgon will leave mineral in place of air.

When this star makes love to the horizon all will be made clear,
Don't question your demons when asked to reveal them,
Perilous this journey during Samhain season,
A rune cast evokes relapse and yet growth has come and passed,
Don't dwell on regrets or you'll choke come time to laugh.

Whisper, don't wake your demons,
There's no reason to free them,
What's said is said, lay me to rest,
You planted the seed,
That took root inside me,
You rid me of my will to live,
My reason to breathe.

Baby, would you please just tell me,
Why I question everything?
And I don't mean you and I,
But, Darling, everything
Makes me want to cry,
The clouds in the sky,
And the birds in the trees,
The fact that I feel fucking nothing,
Or far, far too much.

Woke up, noose around my neck,
'Cut me down', I beg and beg,
As the twines robbing me of air,
I reflect on a life spent losing to fear.

Statued by transparency,
The secrets of Rome reside in marble.

If you were to die, Darling,
I'd throw myself atop this knife,
A romantic's suicide,
Whatever it takes to be back at your side.

Defeated by my envy,
Wretched, putrid, foul,
Empty out your stomach,
Spew your fucking soul,
The grief will not be brief,
When you pay into make-believe.
So, fill me with your poison,
And undress me with deceit.

Why is it I can't find my body weight?
It fucking ran away for its life,
The day I fucked my fucking life.
That's right,
Sleep tight,
Your dreams are out of reach, and then you die.
I smell of sweat,
You smell of sex,
We both give off a scent of fermentation.
Can't remember what we bought,
Though it burnt and we got fucked up,
We forgot all our problems,
Though we're bursting at the seams.

I've been stealing from all my friends,
Their time is worth so much more,
Than my failed attempt at breath,
But still I speak,
I play on repeat,
Tell me, why do I drink when I'm all alone?
Tell me, why do I puke when I'm lonely?

Decipher these words for me,
I can't escape your metaphors,
But I can tell you what hurt worst—
The calls you never answered,
They ultimately led to my hearse.

Come one, come all to the colloquial gathering,
A mass charade of sleight of hand indecency,
Self-appointed importance that squanders love so frequently,
Belittles a throne so befitting of its king.

Well, Darling, the way you hypnotize,
Enough to make any man need an alibi,
So, stop telling me I'm everything,
When I can't stand being anything,
But shut in.
The floorboards whisper,
I can't, I can't, I can't get out my head,
I can't, I can't see not in red,
For my blood boils while my heart rests frozen,
This barrel is bitter,
And my head explosive.

With everything we've been through,
Is it so hard to believe that I still care?

Don't think about the process,
Just carry your weight,
Yeah, 'cause the train never came and the heel toe's leaving late,
You say you want to be a bigger man,
So do I,
So do I, so do I,
I want to be a better person,
All in time,
'Cause these spins keeping me down,
Got me spilling my guts,
Oh,
The bottle came with crutch.

And just like that I'm left in a moment,
Suspended, I'm broken,
If I'd known it would end this way,
I'd do it all again.

Ignorance frequently begets confidence,
Watch the silk spin to gold as you fabricate bliss,
The mind of man is ever at war with invading madness,
So don't believe what you hear and only trust half of what you see.

We know that we're unsafe here,
Yet we slow dance on the spot,
Whispers of a haunting presence,
Skeletons clad in calamity's cloth,
We haven't that much time, Dear,
I feel his presence — Death,
I've longed for you since our first passing,
I can't get you out of my head.

Bewildered by your beauty,
Lips of crimson red,
The pale and cold complexion reminiscent of the dead.
I'd bow to every whim for her,
I'd bleed until I'm bled,
A member of your favourite cellar,
A chalice of your favourite blend.

Darling, know I bite my tongue,
To preserve the peace,
To think you always take for granted
What you hold over the deceased,
So, I bite and bite and bite,
As you talk and talk and talk,
I begin to drown in my own blood,
As not a minute rounds the clock.

I'm sure every word sounds perfect in your fucking head,
But I'm the sorry asshole on the other end.

A whisper in a dream ignites like gasoline,
Eradicating everything in front of me.

I guess I've been struggling to find the words,
I get nervous and choke on my tongue,
But, Babe, please, before you leave, won't you just promise me
You'll stay in case I find them at the bottom of this bottle?
'Cause I couldn't live with myself,
If I just let you walk away.

I remember a time when I found happiness in headaches from the morning light.

So, if I place the trigger next my temple,
Leave my life's work projected cross the wall,
I do not doubt there would be tears,
Just that they'd all be sincere.

Eyelids open,
Yet they are not my own,
For I have grown unfamiliar with the lifeless corpse that
Vacates these sheets.

I'm so terrified of getting back to that point
That I've fabricated this illusion that I'm okay,
That everything is all right and that I'm happy,
When in reality, my stem has been fractured,
I'm left here broken,
Reaching, grasping, clasping for a breath of life,
Anything to keep me moving.
God, could you just give me something to make coping
With the fact that I've opened my eyes for another day
Just a little fucking easier?
To ease the existential terror that comes along with that realization,
Because I am terrified,
And this brown paper bag is the speakeasy that I pour my soul into,
This bottle is Novocain,
My depression, absolute,
And this fucking cigarette is self-conclusion.
End the pain,
Low chemical brain.

What happens when I get tired of faking?
'Cause, honestly, this shit's debilitating.
I've got each of my meds keeping me in bed,
All I've got to do is put a bullet in my head,
But I care too much about those I love.
Yeah, I don't want to break anyone trying to figure my shit out,
And I swear to God, I'd end it all,
But my mom and my dad don't deserve it,
They've been there from the start,
Every fucking problem, they've heard it.
40s on the back deck for lunch,
It's my own fault my stomach feels like shit.

Eyes sewn shut, I'll admit that it's messy,
The voices in my head had my soul undressing,
I was quick to attest, but from lack of rest,
Answered yes to the devil's request to possess.
Repent,
Repent,
This is fucking torment!

Choking on my own teeth, the fucking nosebleeds,
If there really were a God, why would he not intervene?
I'm not a weak man,
But I've got an ill mind,
Pick the scab until it bleeds, then dowse myself in iodine!
Paranoia, I don't mind,
I dowse myself in iodine.

Pry open your mind,
Stop being a martyr.

The maggots feast away inch by inch,
They peel away the flesh on instinct.
You're running out of air but you can't help but scream,
Praying to God this is all just a dream.

Microdosing cyanide to try and kill the pain inside.

Where do you run,
Till you know where to hide?
When it feels like the hills have eyes,
And you've run out of the happiness they've prescribed,
You're not ready to die,
To say goodbye,
Tell me,
Where do I hide?

Darling, please stop hanging on to you and I,
I've broken every fucking promise and I didn't even bat an eye,
I can't stop, won't stop fracturing our love,
I'm hooked, hands down,
The chase to me is like a drug.

Sever ties or be defused,
For a final breath we're gasping,
Catalogue our love's descent,
You rancid bitch, you're nasty.

She locked eyes with me,
And instinctively,
Whispered, 'No one gets out alive,
We may as well live free.'

Scratch,
Expose the cell,
You've got an itch, a give, a tell,
And nobody thinks you wear it well.

Reflection less the prophet suffers,
A conclusion non-divine,
The armada struck true, bringing mass genocide,
A world enflamed,
Everything you loved decimated.

The bottom of the bottle, devil's advocate,
Talked me into popping these pills and slitting my wrists.
Caption every move that I make,
And obliterate
Every ounce of worth that I hold.
This shotgun will spill my last words across the wall.

A cosmic dissonance,
A static discord,
A rift wedged between,
An uninspired daddy's girl,
And a broken boy,
Just trying to survive.

I'll bury you in the ground,
Everything you love will burn,
Of that I'll make sure.
Wrap your mouth around this brimstone ledge,
I want to hear you fucking beg,
'Cause with the kick of a leg,
You'll surely be dead.

This is the end,
Severed ties with everyone that never bent,
While I broke,
Juggling my vices,
I'm ignoring my crisis,
Through this ignorance I'll find bliss.

I demand you bring to light,
Everything you've buried deep,
Spread it out on the table,
And leave me to feast.

Is there anything more haunting than silence,
More terrifying than being left alone with one's thoughts?
For it's in this moment your madness breaks through,
In this moment the beast will cage you,
As a captive you'll be set free,
It's all sin or there is no glory,
Even callous will bleed,
Just like cancer,
Always feeds.

Sometimes we just need a push,
To remind ourselves of the courage we've held this far.
I'd never heard triumph over tragedy,
When I did, it burrowed deep,
Made its way into my scars,
A makeshift heart worn on my sleeve,
Even in death, I will not face defeat.

Playing search 'n' destroy with napalm hearts,
Passing off secrets and filling their scars,
Tucking rain away for sunny days,
Choking on these pills that go down like hand grenades.
Semtex smiles birth explosive truths,
If you'd said it from the start
Then I never would have hurt you.

When all is said and done and the dust has settled,
Will it be for the better?

Confident as self-conscious comes.

I don't know which hurts more—
Not having you here or not knowing,
Not knowing if I'm to blame for your absence.
If I'm at fault for our falling out,
When, really, I'm just happy you're alive,
And if I'd known with me around you were struggling to find
Yourself, I would have walked away,
But only if you'd asked.

Silent sinister and seamless,
Whispers on the wind,
Tonight, the halls will echo
Of lust, of pain, of sin.
The blood will pour as so as wine,
Ecstasy for sober minds,
Leeches peel, what's reaped is sewn,
The only ounce that's lost is hope.

I keep losing my goddamn mind,
Half the time I'm designed to fail,
I'm so fucking frail,
Wish I had an appetite but I'm not hungry,
Fuck, I'm wasting away.

These days, anything that I put down,
Has a proof you need some proof?
My bedsheets covered in puke,
I'm a mess, I need some help.
Save me from distillate hell,
If my liver doesn't give out,
My lungs surely will,
'Cause this cancer is so addicting,
Open vein, rinse, repeat.

I've got my eye on the back door,
Don't kick it in, kick it in,
No,
The shades kiss bleak silence,
Subconscious goes violent as I'm reminded,
This mediocrity is all I'll ever know.

I don't know why I fall asleep outside sometimes,
I don't know why I cut myself
Down a size,
Or why, when I drink, I finally feel alive.
Could it be that I'm nothing special?
Could it be that I just get carried away?
From time to time, the thought bleeds true,
From time to time, from high to high,
Sure, I had my demons
But I killed them from the inside.

I had high hopes,
As in I got high and hoped things would get better.
I never weathered the storm,
Just took it head-on from the back seat.
I'm in the passenger's seat,
Yet the driver looks just like me.

I may be mad, but I'm certain of uncertainty,
So, learn to steer with our failure and fill our sails,
For I am the royal we.

Sometimes I close my eyes and hold my breath,
Forget the existential dread,
The songbirds whisper to the sombre dead,
I'll burn this place to the ground
Just to silence my skeletons.

For the weight of the world, is a bullet the cure?

Being dead has its benefits,
In Hell, I never need a light for my cigarette.

If the reaper has my name and it's time,
Hurry it up, I'm burning out in my prime.

Let's hear it for the tragic youth,
Who gave up on themselves before the world could let them down,
The broken teenage dreams bursting at the seams,
'Cause you're no surgeon, you're no seamstress,
Yet you administered your treatment,
'Cause you refused to give anyone a reason,
A reason to worry,
But now you're drowning in the shallows,
Spending every other day swept away by the ocean waves,
Maybe my hope will return,
Go off like a grenade and explode,
Destroying everything that made me choke.

You ever just think about ending it all?
About fucking off so far, the next star can't see,
'Cause we surrendered our world to scum,
And they made it an equal sum,
Of all fears, my greatest is falling short, or running out of beer,
'Cause I can't do what I do on a sober mind,
Sick and tired all the time and I'm an ass,
Botanist Phoenix,
I rose from the ash.

I use this bottle like a crowbar,
Tear down all the walls I placed there,
Just to face the people who care.
I'm a rabbit in a snare,
So quick,
So unaware.

I can give up on anything if I'm left
Alone with my thoughts long enough.
I'm a self-cynic, chemically imbalanced — ask the clinic,
The only time I'm happy is when I'm winning,
Sinning, or fucking singing.
God, if you could just liquidate this self-hate,
Relieve me of grieving,
Just put a bullet in this parasitic feeling.

Choking on the words that fill my mouth but never vacate.

I won't consecrate the shrine,
Open vein bleeding dry,
Like a split-lip, spit-fist massacre,
I brought my conscience to a gun fight.

Why am I so insignificant?
Will I break before I find myself again?

How sweet is the affection of others to a wretch like I?
Now there's nothing left but
A melody, sewn deep within a memory
That you gave to me.
You replaced my love with anguish in its entirety,
You cut me open just to see if I would bleed.

The fact that I'm unhappy but you're happy makes me cry.

Well, I was 26 years old
When I found out breaking someone's heart
Hurt far worse than
A broken heart itself—
At least to me.

Just when you've stopped believing things will work out
And that you'll find happiness,
The world surprises you with something that you've
hoped so long for.

When you're clueless, waiting on a sign,
The fear of missing it will eat at you alive,
'Cause I'm going on a decade waiting for you, Dear,
So please, don't hold your tongue
If you're wanting to be near
Someone like me.
Maybe it's me,
But I won't get my hopes up
Just to drown them out at sea.
Someone like me,
A memory,
I never fully gave up hope,
Our roads again would meet.

Hung out with her most of the day, then we got dinner,
It feels so good spending time with her again.
I wish time didn't go by so fast when were together,
Which is strange, because lately, I've been
In a perpetual state of fast-forward.
I need to slow everything down around me,
Take in every day for what it is.

Complications go hand in hand with growth,
Don't cut yourself down before your ground is even cultivated.

Brimstone has a particular smell,
So, tell me, Darling, why are you drenched in the scent of Hell?

Rural depression won't make nest 'neath my bones,
Despite this murder stalking over,
This parasite will not feast on an imbalance yet deceased,
Lay the salt, strike a match, burn the witch, repent the act.
In God's, eyes we're nothing more than porcelain pariahs,
A calloused hand, burnt while starting these fires.
Cleanse your soul, break free from hate to retire,
Weep for the willows and the Lord's fallen child.

I found out the hard way that critics manufacture cynics,
I bear witness to a decimated instant,
Uncertainty certainly never sunk its teeth
Beneath this facade,
And yet I'm humbled by the opportunity just to be myself.

Mark my words, I'll put an end to greed,
Light a cigarette and do away with thee,
Bottle o' bourbon hope on yer breath,
An' a petrified heart still beating outta yer chest.
It's the Deadman Walking Blues,
Gave it all up just to have 'em all grovel at you,
The Deadman Walking Blues,
You got cross, went in on a toss,
Sonny boy, you met the devil, made a gamble
And lost.

Sometimes you wake up,
Catch wind of sorrow,
And completely give up hope.

To the optimist, ever on the bright side,
I commend thee,
For the ability to find beauty on this God-forsaken mineral is in itself immense,
As I cannot find a single molecule worthy of instilling hope,
Not when this decrepit land knows only of decay.

The scent of downpour finds itself entangled in this web
Of air I breathe,
And yet I disassociate from this subtle saunter breeze,
Placed before my eyes
To please,
Yet still I sleep,
Just let me sleep.

Distorted dictation weighing on my impatience,
Christianity will conquer due to the walking brainless.

Bow your head and take a knee, all ye with forked tongues,
To the pacifists we anarchists are all but legal terrorists,
Draping cigarette-stained flesh over calloused hands
Once sleepy eyes have said goodnight.
Thoughts are so often misconstrued during consumption
And, Darling, I was under the assumption that your heart,
Well, it would forever beat in time with mine.
Then I convinced myself you're lying,
'Cause I've dismantled enough second-hand spider webs
Sewn deep with meaning and sincerity,
To procreate and fertilize the idea
That you never truly cared for me,
A pawn forever beneath its queen,
I only beg you never ask,
"Go forth and die for me."

Describe for me the beauty buried deep within
Melancholy,
The madness that cloaks itself beneath this veil of
Veracity,
Display on a canvas for me the ideologies that compose
Your very existence,
The introspection and confidence turbulently kneading
My nerves until
Mentality and perception bleed cohesively into
Retrospective imagery,
Once again revealing some semblance of peace.

They say, "Be sure to reach out, check in on your friends,"
The planet is dying we're facing the end,
So yes, I'm depressed, and about quite a bit,
But "How're you doing?"— it doesn't fix shit.

Grieving for the sake of feeling anything,
I've sewn my shadow to my soul.
Where do you turn when the walls are bleeding?
Where do I look when I catch the ceiling staring back?
Ugh,
I've found my way through hell just fine on my own,
Tell me, why does everything that I've grown feel clinical?
It's hypothetical but what if we weren't so cynical
Towards the world?
We could build a life in our own image.
A shoe that fits us,
Would be disastrous.

When the end appears before our sleepless eyes,
Would we take a bow and give up, would we fight?
'Cause I've been rolling over every night,
Questioning the man I am deep down inside,
The more and more I ponder what it is to be,
The less and less I see a point to breathe,
Still I smile, and approach life with
All too eager a disposition.
Don't take my lack of attention to heart,
Darling, it's gotten me this far.

We flew kites past coffee shops and tied our shoes together,
I can still hear us laughing
At how sad the entirety of existence is.
We'd get high and swim in our thoughts,
Our depleting sanity,
Composing symphony upon symphony,
Elegance garnered our infamy.

Don't wait,
'Cause I don't want to be around
When they discover you,
'Cause I'm the one who buried you,
The very one who married you,
Will our secret ever sleep?
Why do you call to me?
Stalking the mezzanine,
Oh, so impatiently,
Calling me home.

And if I took myself out there would be no doubt that I
Loved myself,
No doubt that I'm not broken,
I'm just an anomaly searching for a long-lost wonder,
A spacetime lover,
Designed to fit cohesively to me.

The one person I longed to spend this day with
Spent it with someone else they call their own.

I drink to forget, then forget to forget.

Will I crawl out of here?
Will I peel the nail from my bone?
Will I spin silk of gold?
Take my life to drown the echo,
I've already let go.

Caught myself tugging at a single breath,
Reaching out at every word,
Searching deeply in myself,
To bring to light a little goddamn life,
So sick of waking up at noon and feeling dead inside,
I want life,
I need to feel alive,
So terrified, petrified that I will die,
I simply let happiness pass me by.

Cancerous this betrayal leaves me concussed,
Seeing stars, the bars refuse to heal all scars,
So, to hell with this sober state of mind,
I've got to get back,
Barkeep,
Re-wine, remind, rewind.

It feels nice,
Knowing in the grand scheme of things,
That I could die tomorrow, and the world wouldn't be
Any better or worse off than it was,
There's just something so comforting about being
invisible.

What is it about your clothes that makes me want to tear
Them off?
Whoa.
Tell me, Dear, is it you who haunts my soul?
For I've spent countless sleepless nights
Begging you to go,
Just to find the morning sun kept rising without hope,
For I am not a holy man,
But I have been through hell,
I triumphed every crucible,
And drank from every well.

We wipe our hands of past mistakes,
Then build our throne on yesterday.

You caught me off guard when you said you missed me,
Like a rabid dog, I was hungry for a reason to settle down,
But you
Just
Kept
Hanging around.
This poverty line's looking mighty high,
When the path of success is born out of sight.
Don't be impatient.
It's off-putting,
And just like everything important,
I'm putting you off.

When all is said and done
And I've permanently wiped this smile from existence,
Remember every single time you said you'd never miss it,
'Cause I've been pulling rabbits out my heart
Trying not to fall apart.
Forgive me, but,
If this is living, when do I start?

3am, wide awake, not a drop of booze in me,
It's hard to sleep,
I smoke again, I think anxiety's winning.
When we die, where do we go?
I find myself wondering,
Will I paint the sunset gold and catch myself smiling?
'Do not disturb' screens all my calls,
So lately I don't feel sorry at all,
I'm not in the mood, not in the mind,
So hang up the phone—
Just stop fucking trying.

If you're afraid, don't hesitate,
Turn to the lights and let them guide you home,
This could be anything,
The cancer cuts, it bleeds the truth,
Caught in the path of your own troubled youth,
Despicable,
Unbearable,
A sad man's sob story parable,
Even a gutted gull screams if its lungs are full.

If somebody lives partially in fantasy to get by,
Who are we do destroy such a construct?
In this world the fact anyone can find happiness
Is beautiful enough,
Don't shit on it because you hate your nine to five
And Netflix routine.

We normalized laughing at others' failures,
Simultaneously destroying our will to try.

Maybe one day I'll explain
The imprint that you left on my heart,
Here's to hoping,
'Cause without you I won't get very far.
You've plagued my dreams for years,
Waking up to no you and tears.
One day I'll tell you everything,
Maybe by then I won't be broken.

We've all been there before,
All had a dance with death at our door,
Well, death made peace beneath my sheets,
And left me wanting more.

When it's all said,
And it's all sad,
Where is it we'll end up?
Oh, 'cause this soul was battered,
When your lips were kissed,
Oh, this heart was broken,
When you said yes.

Maybe I'm just a fool,
For everything and nothing,
But, Darling, everything
Leaves me feeling nothing,
And nothing
Leaves me wanting everything but you.

So please, sink your teeth into me,
Go on girl, take a bite,
This evening will haunt all my dreams,
I'm paralyzed,
So sink your sink your teeth into me,
For even in this waking hell,
True love is permanent.

Weeping now, the angels know they've lost,
I've been seduced, in the devil I will trust,
For as the walls watch, I pledge my life to thee,
Till death or victory,
I'll impale all your enemies.

So go on, hush up, Darling,
My ears began to bleed,
Everything you've never gotten,
Is everything you claim to need.

You sent today at 17:25,
To everyone I've let down, please know
It's eating me alive,
I've crawled too far within myself,
These walls are where I hide.
I love you all so dearly,
And I don't want to cause you grief,
My descent into madness overpowered my belief
That beggars can't be choosers,
A castle wasn't meant for swine,
Wave goodbye to Dr Jekyll,
And fucking welcome Mr Hyde.

For the greatest of empaths will always admire those with apathy.

Can't take much more of this, Darling,
I've fought through thick and thin, believing everything
Would eventually work out
But it won't,
So where does that leave us?
I'm terrified that our interwoven souls
Will fracture upon separation,
For I've no memory of the man I was before this,
Every piece of my being that I can say I'm proud of,
Was cultivated by your touch.

Why is it I'm unable to move,
Despite the capability of moving forward?
Is it possible I'm happy?
Or have I simply become a recluse,
Creating fantasy in words to avoid the fragility of it all?
I think I'll lay down for a while.

I'd forgotten the confines of this mind grow dreary
When met head-on with overwhelming nothingness.
This boredom presents itself
As a voice internally omnipotent,
And I'm once again convincing myself that I'm a chore.

For I will never do away with self-sabotage,
Not until the day I can truly say I want to be here.

I've imagined for a while, one night I'll expire,
I'll close my eyes and cease to breathe,
Then I'll haunt my memories,
I'll take a look at the man I used to be,
And I don't mean who I presented,
But deep down who I was when it truly counted,
The man that I was when it came down to the wire,
When push came to shove, regardless of how tired
The man I was,
And I'd be lying if I said
That this would be peaceful recompense,
Due to heartbreak and over-the-counter medicine,
I still remember the year the existential dread kicked in.

You've got to promise me right now
You won't do what they say.
All the eyes do is listen,
Despite averting their gaze.
They want to dissect your honour,
Then sign and dot your toe-tag,
They'll take your morals to market,
Butchered and cut with low grade.

The transient passion you displayed
Filled my heart and then brought pain,
Brought so much hope and so much rain,
I'm drowning in our yesterdays.
Can anyone let slip what went wrong?
These drugs that stole my dreams
Were the supposed authors of a better me,
Oh, the hypocrisy.

You were like no one,
No one I'd ever met before,
Deviant, distant,
Rotten to the core,
Your putrid persona,
Decaying in its pestilence,
To all with eyes that can attest,
Labelled you, antagonist.

You're like a bad drink,
What with how you make me choke,
With how you make my throat burn.

The very force that extended forth and encased me,
Was a feeling of warmth, of love, of clarity,
Wielding passion incarnate,
He fell deeply and madly in love with his own madness,
Questioning only the cruel and insufferable moments
Of sanity, woven through reality.

There's a sad and wretched beast
Rotting 'neath these sheets,
And with the scent of a proof, it reflects how I see
Myself at times, when I'm too fucked up to stand,
And yet I tip the bottle back again,
All because I heard that demons can't swim,
But now I'm convinced the ones who told me that,
Was them.

The complications life presents are non-linear,
So, take the good days when they show themselves,
And take the troubles for what they are—
Temporary.

Wither,
Weep,
Just promise me you'll never worry.

I found myself lost in trying to rationalize
The give and take of life.

Just had the strangest dream…
Before my eyes,
A deconstructed city,
Separated piece by piece,
The good, the bad, the ugly.

As I held your hand in mine,
I tucked a strand of hair behind your ear and whispered,
'My love,
Not until the waves cease to crash,
Nor the mountains kiss the sky,
Will the feelings I feel,
Wither and die.'

The ashes that secretly filled the urn,
Were far more beautiful than any flower
That had once called it home.

I refuse to give up on who I am
In order to please those who never knew who I was.

At such a height, the concrete looks paper thin,
I wonder,
Is this where my story ends,
Or where it begins?

I'll shed the weight that doubt let linger,
And if failure is what my future holds,
I'll shape said failure into home.

And though I love the chase,
Nothing compares to your lipstick just below my waist.

As I struggle to talk myself out of bed,
Words pop into my head,
Desperate to get them down, I lose track of time,
What was I doing
Prior to this line?
"Diamonds disguise land mines."

I'm ashamed that I'm incapable of simply asking
If you're all right,
But, Darling, don't mistake my silence for negligence,
For not a moment passes
That I am unaware of my cowardice.
Please know that I am being slaughtered,
That I am losing a war with demons
I long thought drank sequestered.

So sorely mistaken,
This eye for an eye means no more than the forsaken,
So, cast not your stones but the unparalleled hope,
That love, and love alone,
Will deliver us home.

This littered trail of unwrapped thoughts,
Undressed for me the Devil's God,
Marauding masked, I'd seek the sought,
I'd walked until I leapt distraught,
I left my love in pieces,
A glistening amalgamation of brain and concrete,
Dismantled at your feet.

Deter the thoughts, of plague, of doom,
Of all dark spirits haunting you,
Then cry out to your mother moon,
With this sacrifice we bring to you,
We offer up our gratitude.
Bless our sons, our daughters, too,
Bless the air that fills our lungs,
And dowse the fires from which we run.

Despite all of your efforts,
I'm breaking down once again,
A scribbled note composed of hope,
Read like symphonies of old,
Melodic silence chemical,
The secrets of Rome reside in marble.

We celebrate illusion,
Then break our bodies as if bread,
We beg to thee, rife with defeat,
To spare us from calamity,
With sharpened blade we draw blood,
Mark all five points and speak, speak up,
My Lord who dwells in darkness,
Through no fault of thy own,
I call to you with soul intact,
I offer entrance to my home,
Come forth to me thy demons,
Come forth and offer me thy hand,
Let my writing reach the world,
Then let me perish with the dammed.

We're just pacing on matches,
Blacking out words until it's all redacted,
Hoarding the truth that could set us free,
Crippling the youth with debt and insecurity.

Frozen in a construct non-linear,
Terrified to fuck up,
I find all of my strength within fear.
Call it cynicism, whatever you will,
But this cataclysm will spawn negligence
And even the biggest hearts will read,
'Off with their heads.'

For even a free spirit, at times, purchases and
Locks their own shackles

Hope will always survive in those who continue to fight.
I believe in you,
As I always have,
And I believe in whom you choose to replace me,
Your memories,
You erased them for me,
Failure is not the end,
It's a necessary part of the path.

For if writing cannot save my life,
I know not what will.

Breathe deep,
Hold it,
Hold it,
Release.

He watched as time took prisoner of all he held dear.

Wandering spirits simply seek understanding.
When they force goosebumps upon you,
They simply want someone to know
The fear that gripped them the moment before they died,
That very moment before they forever shut their eyes.

Can you drag the weeping lake?
Its sinister whispers have, without a doubt,
Caught my influenced ear,
And yet my boney knees continue to carry my naked soul,
With feet turned black from last night's snow.
Lost.
I've been lost for so long,
Trying to make circles out of squares,
Trying to make sense of my life,
To realize I don't care.
I long for the feeling of your lips upon my brow,
And the soothing nothingness I feel when you tell me
"Everything will be all right".
You left, though,
Abandoned me and my self-doubt,
To self-medicate and eat away at my sanity.
I'm lost without you,
So just as the tide pulled you under,
And kept you for itself,
Will it wash away my sorrow,
And drown me of self-doubt?
I miss you,
I love you,
I'll see you soon.
Her body caught my eye,
While her essence tackled my soul,
If there was any doubt about if she were the one,
My boney knees hold the answer.

I stop myself from falling into an endless abyss,
At the same time, I'm the one who got myself here,
And I'm curious to see where it takes me,
For this hole I've dug myself is reminiscent
Of the hole inside my chest,
And the sparrow lodged inside my lungs,
Leaves me short for breath,
But it sounds so beautiful.

I keep telling myself to catch myself before I slip,
But your words leave me intoxicated,
They leave me on a high every time you say goodnight,
And every time I say good morning.

From where does this depression stem,
When I recognize fully and accept that we are
But dust from stars?
And why do I keep bandaging these wounds
With four-dollar pints in the bell of these shitty bars?

The oak I rest my elbows upon,
Is the only thing left keeping me up,
So. as I finish the happiness from this cup,
I begin to feel empty,
And as I surrender my bones to emptiness,
I get lost in euphoria.
I just can't seem to get my head out of the clouds,
God knows I'd break my neck to avoid this haze,
But I'm holding on for dear life to the past,
Biting down on yesterday
And draining it of everything that made it
Special in the first place.

It's in the way your lips collide when you speak,
And the way the lies push past your forked tongue.
Was deception always your intention,
Or is there the slightest of possibilities that,
For once in my life,
I actually meant something to someone?

The ghost of addiction is one that never fades,
So your cigarettes,
Shit whiskey,
And fragile heart will continue to weigh you down.
But if you're happy with your head under water,
Fuck it,
There has always been an underlying beauty
In self destruction.

The debris my life has created has me climbing
Over obstacles from many a yesterday.
Just because I've pushed past the past before,
Doesn't mean it can't still cripple me.
It shouldn't,
But that hasn't stopped it from doing so yet.

It's never easy opening yourself up,
And letting your soul bleed out over the page.
But then again,
Nothing beautiful has ever been easy.

It never gets easier,
Looking around for someone to find console in,
Only to remember you're alone,
The same as yesterday,
The same as tomorrow,
Alone with no one to subside your sorrow,
Not a person with an ounce of happiness free to borrow.

For once,
I wish someone would realize I'm alone
Because I'm trying to make friends.

Sometimes tolerance can become intolerable,
So why do you put up with me
If even the way I breathe drives you crazy?
If I'm the reason you grind your teeth,
Then I'm the reason you weep,
For your headaches have returned to plague you,
Headaches you can't just sleep through.
So if saying goodbye is what's best for you,
I'll save you the trouble—
Adieu.

Every day, tomorrow seems a struggle,
As if each and every morning
I've recycled yesterday's exhaustion and nausea.
Dismantled under this spell,
How can I look forward to tomorrow's heaven
If I can't see passed todays crippling hell?

I appreciate your existence
And the way you positively impact my life
Just by being you.

So many lies have made their way past your lips,
That every word you've had me believe,
Ends up leaving me in disbelief,
For you threw me from the wall I so comfortably sat atop,
Leaving me to pick myself up, piece by piece.
So forgive me if I'm hesitant to hear your plea,
Forgive me for not wanting to hear 'I'm sorry,'
Because, Darling,
I know you're not,
Not really.

The truth is, you had my trust,
Then you abandoned it the way you abandoned me.
You made the incision in my ventral cavity,
And stole every ounce of vitality.
I'm drowning,
Shallow,
Hollow,
Alone,
Choking on something I once called home.

Grow with me,
Or don't.
Reach for tomorrow with me,
Or hold on to the past.
Pick me up, or tear me down,
Just promise me you'll never leave me alone
With my thoughts.

I watch as your emotions slow dance,
And applaud your moment of happiness,
Tranquility,
A gift whose kiss you've not felt for so long,
That it's as if I were watching two old friends meet again
At the end of a lifetime,
Instantly becoming transparent,
No secrets,
No holding back,
Just the warm embrace if an old friend's kind words.
So don't tell me I'm wasting my time
Trying to free you from depression,
When your very smile allows me escape from my own.

She was an angel,
Hell-bent on resting with the Devil.

The moment my eyes fell upon you
And we caught each other's gaze,
I knew you were a gift from the heavens.
Now that the euphoria has passed,
I'm finally willing to accept that your true intentions
Were hiding beneath a mask,
And sadly,
It was the mask I had fallen in love with.

Panic ensues in the minds of the confused,
Perpetually consuming,
The negative in everything that leaves them bruised,
Blinded now by phantom beauty,
They continue to leave themselves open,
Susceptible to the negativity again and again,
Until they begin to buckle,
Asphyxiated,
Isolated,
Helplessly searching for the happiness they once held,
Only to realize it wasn't stolen,
That from being so malnourished and neglected,
It had simply transmuted.
What no one will ever tell you, though,
Is that the only place you'll find
That transfigured happiness
Is within yourself,
It's just lying dormant
Until the day you once again decide to love yourself.

Do things for yourself,
Smile because you fucking can,
Get drunk on a Monday,
High on a Tuesday,
Watch a movie alone, or go out and make love,
There is so much beauty neglected
By those who admire it,
Because they're afraid of what iconoclasts may think.
Fuck what they think.
After all,
A wise man once said,

Being invisible isn't that bad,
It's getting erased that hurts.

Just think about it,
Think about every time she ever made you smile,
Every time she ever made you feel worthwhile,
Think about how she held you together while you were
Eroding beneath depression,
Then ask yourself if the girl your friends call crazy
Is really worth letting go of.

Shower away the booze and stale cigarettes
You poisoned yourself with during last night's bender.
Surrender every ounce of dignity
You've managed to hold on to after twenty-two years,
And break a piece away.
Because I swear, the one thing etched into our minds
Growing up,
Was to be ourselves, no matter what.
Was that a lie?
For the last time, I look in the mirror before heading out the door,
I remember thinking,
Who am?

I'm sorry I missed your calls,
I really wish that I hadn't,
Because knowing in the moment
You were thinking of me,
I was absent minded of you,
It kills me.
I was unable to console you,
To say whatever words you needed to hear,
Regardless of how simple they may have been,
And I love you.
Are you okay?
I miss you too.
I'm on my way.
Whatever you were seeking, I was unable to provide,
And that is why I will never deserve you.

With my windows down,
I could still hear the sound of angels weeping,
Yet I was begging,
Seeking guidance from somewhere,
Besides that in which I don't believe.
I found comfort in a bottle,
I neglected every other option,
And that is where my problem stems from,
My dependence on a percentage for help.

A hanging head so easy to pass by,
A lover's tryst so easy to forget,
What is it about today's youth that makes
Finding a good thing bad?
And why do they turn their backs on love?
It's a gift,
Embrace it.

People are individuals.
To seclude yourself to a stereotype is limiting.

Trouble calls my name in a familiar voice,
Destruction with apathy always kills my poise.
You stole my words when you removed my tongue,
You burned my world
Like the love of my lung from these cigarettes.

If I'd known you were passing me your hell, I would have accepted it,
You didn't need to end it all,
You just needed to ask for help.

Darling, if I'd known these dark thoughts
Plague you all the time,
I'd have done my best to rip them from your mind,
To set you free from the crippling thoughts,
Killing the heart I've come to love.
But I was so invested in myself I couldn't tell,
I never noticed the immeasurable amount
Of shit you were going through,
And if I'd known that I could have saved you,
Maybe the events of that night
Never would have gone through.
Maybe I'd still have you.
Maybe this God-forsaken world would still have you,
And maybe my life never would have met this standstill.
If I'd have known you were going to pass me your hell,
I would have accepted it.
You didn't need to end it all,
You just needed to ask for help.
If I'd known you were passing me your hell,
I would have taken your hand
And told you that we'd make it,
I would have taken your hand and held on.
But there's no point in what-ifs,
Because of all the angels, you shine the brightest,
And of all the angels,
You're the one my heart is with,
You're the one I'll always miss.

There's an irrational obsession
With fixing that which is not broken.
In doing so, there is a strange sort of irony,
Because so often,
Aimlessly seeking perfection
Is that which breaks us.

I'm tired of feeling like an abscess,
I'm sick of people taking advantage of others
Because their ideologies say it's okay.
It isn't,
Stop being a cunt.

Peel me like bark on a tree,
Show me the parts of myself only you find seemly,
For self-doubt clouds my mind,
And I question who I am all the time.
The thing that amazes me, though,
Is that even though I've no idea the type of person I am,
The best in me is all you're willing to see.

I watched her dance in death's frigid arms,
Tripping over the way she embraced its kiss,
The way she got on with something so cold and dead
Was absolutely mesmerizing.
Unfortunately, in the end,
It left even her breathless.

Been wandering,
Losing myself on purpose,
For the thrill,
For the fall,
For that shot of adrenaline,
The moment I realize that I'm dead again,
It's the moment I realize I can do anything,
Be anyone,
I can shape myself in the same way God hypothetically
Shaped all of his children.
My path is mine and mine alone,
And if I choose to get lost and wander the unknown,
Not a soul can stop me.

Sometimes I wonder if my vulgar skeleton gets tired of
Being dragged around by my manic soul.

www.ingramcontent.com/pod-product-compliance
Lightning Source LLC
LaVergne TN
LVHW091544060526
838200LV00036B/703